DIY Projects & Gift Ideas for Mother's Day

By: Do It Yourself Nation

Copyright © 2015 by Do It Yourself Nation

All rights reserved. No part of this book may be reproduced in any form without permission in writing from the author. Reviewers are able to quote brief passages in reviews.

Disclaimer

This document is geared towards providing exact and reliable information in regards to the topic and issue covered. The publication is sold with the idea that the publisher is not required to render accounting, officially permitted, or otherwise, qualified services. If advice is necessary, legal or professional, a practiced individual in the profession should be ordered.

- From a Declaration of Principles which was accepted and approved equally by a Committee of the American Bar Association and a Committee of Publishers and Associations.

In no way is it legal to reproduce, duplicate, or transmit any part of this document in either electronic means or in printed format. Recording of this publication is strictly prohibited and any storage of this document is not allowed unless with written permission from the publisher. All rights reserved.

The information provided herein is stated to be truthful and consistent, in that any liability, in terms of inattention or otherwise, by any usage or abuse of any policies, processes, or directions contained within is the solitary and utter responsibility of the recipient reader. Under no circumstances will any legal responsibility or blame be held against the publisher for any reparation, damages, or monetary loss due to the information herein, either directly or indirectly.

Respective authors own all copyrights not held by the publisher.

The information herein is offered for informational purposes solely, and is universal as so. The presentation of the information is without contract or any type of guarantee assurance.

The trademarks that are used are without any consent, and the publication of the trademark is without permission or backing by the trademark owner. All trademarks and brands within this book are for clarifying purposes only and are the owned by the owners themselves, not affiliated with this document.

Introduction

Do you recall the last time you offered a truly special gift to your mother – one made by your own hands? Do you worry you're not creative enough to design a truly outstanding gift?

Are you thinking of giving your mom the same gift you offered last year since you can't think of anything better? If you had a child who gave you the same gifts over and over again, how would you feel? Wouldn't you feel unappreciated and taken for granted? Wouldn't you feel exhilarated to get a handmade gift from your son or daughter? So would your mother!

If you are looking to try your hand in making handmade gifts for your mother, then you are in the right place. This book is all you need to put a smile on your mother's face this Mother's Day because it's full of amazing gift ideas that you can craft for your mother. They range from jewelry, clothes and accessories and food gifts to home décor and other amazing gift ideas. If you want to surprise your mom, in a good way, this is the perfect book for you.

About This Book

This book is divided into six chapters where different designs and gifts ideas are suggested. The first chapter has gift ideas for pampering your mother. We know women love being pampered, so pamper her today and put a smile on her face! The second chapter illustrates various projects for improving home décor, while the third chapter discusses ways of designing unique jewelry. The fourth chapter then looks at some ideas for making clothes and accessories and the fifth chapter looks at amazing food gift ideas. The last chapter offers various other kinds of amazing gift ideas that you can try out.

Table of Contents

Introduction — 1

About This Book — 2

Chapter 1: Pampering Gift Ideas — 6

   Lotion Bars — 6

   Chocolate Whipped Body Butter — 7

   Mommy Pampering Kit — 9

   Homemade Pomegranate Facial Scrub — 10

   DIY Lip Balm — 12

   Mint Lime Foot Soak — 14

   Anti-Wrinkle Cream — 15

Chapter 2: Home Décor Gift Ideas — 17

   Birch Bark Candles — 17

   Kitchen Tablet Holder — 18

   Mother's Day Printable — 20

   Tissue Paper Picture Frame — 22

   Family Tree Serving Tray — 24

   Stenciled Tea Towels — 25

Chapter 3: Jewelry Gift Ideas — 29

   T-Shirt Necklace — 29

   Embossed Painted Can Flower — 31

   Bird Nest Necklace — 32

   Painted Wooden Bracelets — 34

   Button Necklace — 35

   DIY Thumbprint Necklace — 39

Mother's Day Succulent Rings	41
Chapter 4: Clothes and Accessories Gift Ideas	**45**
Leather Tassels	45
Doily Canvas Bag	47
DIY Shoe Clips	49
An-Hour Bag Gift	52
Super Easy Summer Dress	59
Infinity Scarf	61
Add Beaded Fringe to Pants	63
Chapter 5: Food Gift Ideas	**65**
Iced Chai Tea Latte Mix	65
Gift Box Cookies	67
Peach Strawberry Butterfly Cake	69
Butterfingers Dip	71
Crêpes with Strawberries and Muscat-Yogurt Sauce	72
Chocolate Brownie Cake	75
Granola with Lots of Dried Fruit	76
Edible Flowers for Mother's Day	78
Chapter 6: Other Gift Ideas	**82**
Fabric Covered Books	82
Fabric Scrap Key Chain	85
Mother's Day Gardening Gift	88
Mason Jar Sewing Kits	90
Threaded Washer Pendant	93
Mod Podge® Lace Vases	95

Recipe Holder Gift Idea	98
Tile Coaster Tutorial	102

Conclusion — 106

Key Takeaways From This Book — 107

How To Put This Information Into Action — 108

Preview of Essential Oils and Aromatherapy: A Beginner's Guide to Making Essential Oils to Improve Your Mental and Physical Well-Being — 109

More Books You Might Like — 111

Your Free Bonus — 112

Chapter 1:
Pampering Gift Ideas

You can make various gifts to pamper your mother this Mother's Day; you can try making lip balm, perfume, bath salts, lotions, and creams. Below are a few ideas to get started:

Lotion Bars

What you'll need

- 4 ounces coconut oil
- 4 ounces Shea butter
- 4.5 ounces beeswax

How to Make

Measure the ingredients or get the pre-measured form and then combine the ingredients in a double boiler. Melt and stir well, and then transfer the molten mixture into molds. You can try using a turkey baster to completely fill the mold with your molten lotion. You can utilize any material to make your own mold, such as metal, plastic, cupcake pans or ice cube trays.

Wait for a moment to allow the lotion materials to completely cool before you pop out or use. To help you remove the lotion bar from the mold, you can freeze the set-up for about 30 minutes before removing.

Chocolate Whipped Body Butter

What you'll need

- 2 tablespoons pure cocoa or cacao powder
- 1-2 teaspoons peppermint essential oil
- ½ cup of jojoba or mild olive oil or almond oil
- ½ cup coconut oil
- ½ cup cocoa butter, organic mango or shea butter
- ½ cup of organic cocoa butter
- 2 teaspoons naturally derived vitamin E, optional

How to Make

Start by making an ice bath. Using ice, fill a large bowl and then fit a small bowl inside. Ensure that the inner bowl has capacity to support about 5 cups of liquid.

Now melt mango butter and cocoa butter in a double boiler or a large bowl that is fitted with a smaller bowl inside. Heat the mixture over and then add in coconut oil. Continue to melt this mixture until it completely turns into liquid. When done, remove the molten mixture from heat.

Into a separate small bowl, measure about 5 teaspoons of cocoa powder and then gradually add several teaspoons of any essential oil; among them olive, almond or jojoba. Mix the oil and cocoa powder and continue to add coconut oil mixture along with the remaining essential oil.

Transfer the mixture into the cooled bowl, placed on an ice bowl. Allow the contents to rest for about 10 minutes. When chilled, remove this mixture from the ice bath and whip to form stiff peaks. If your mixture appears not to thicken, you should return it to the ice bath and whip on ice.

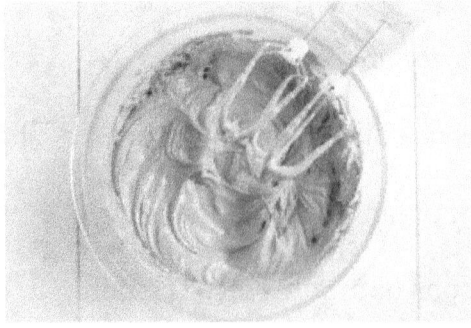

Store the mixture in an airtight jar, preferably cobalt or amber in color, though you can use a clear jar. If using a transparent jar, keep the mixture free from sunlight, which can result in oxidation.

For a longer period of use, use cold-pressed high quality oils to increase the lifetime to 3-6 months. For extra durability, you can use vitamin E to preserve your butter for up to a year.

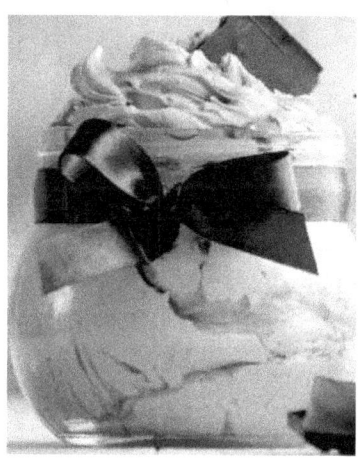

Mommy Pampering Kit

What you'll need

- Plastic bottle, 2-liter capacity
- Gift items
- Tape

How to make

Get a bottle of any capacity (it could be two liters or more/less) then empty and clean it. Make a small opening in the bottle and insert your gift items through it.

Things like chocolate, coffee, mouthwash, lotions, gum, and hand sanitizer are great choices, but be as creative as you want! When done, use a tape to close the opening you made.

Homemade Pomegranate Facial Scrub

Pomegranate oil has excellent anti-wrinkle and anti-oxidant properties for the skin. The oil that fights various skin conditions is found in the pomegranate seeds.

What you'll need

- ½ cup white sugar
- ½ cup pomegranate seeds, crushed with juice
- 2-3 tablespoons of honey

How to make

Slit the fruit open using a sharp knife and pry the halves apart. To make it easier to clean up the deep dark red juice, do this near a sink. Pick the seeds out of the pomegranate with the fruit inside a bowl of water. Submerging it in water allows the seeds to easily sink and the fleshy part to float.

Put some honey into a bowl, add the seeds, and then crush them using a wooden spoon. You may need to use a towel to cover the top of the bowl to prevent the juice from spraying you as you crush the seeds.

To make a scrub, add sufficient amount of sugar and stir. For a thicker scrub, just add more sugar. You can either remove the seeds after juicing them or leave the crushed seeds in the scrub.

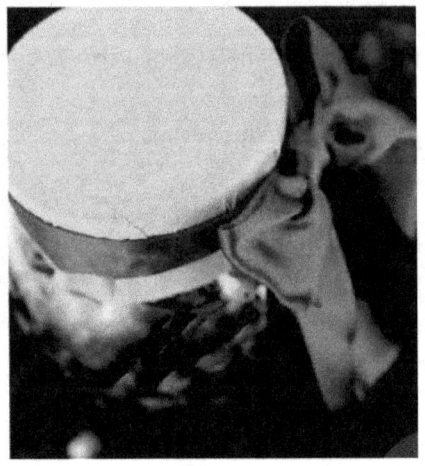

DIY Lip Balm

What you'll need

- 5 ml buttercream cupcake flavor oil
- 2 level tablespoons carnauba wax or beeswax / pastilles wax
- 2 teaspoons coconut oil, fractionated
- ¼ ounce mango butter
- ¼ ounce shea butter
- ¼ ounce cocoa butter
- pinch of matte purple pigment powder
- pinch of diamond dust mica

How to make

On your kitchen scale, weigh out the butters and then mix them in a measuring cup or small glass bowl. Measure 2 level tablespoons of beeswax pellets or grated beeswax and mix it into the butter.

In a double boiler or microwave, melt the beeswax and butters on low heat until liquid, and stir thoroughly to mix.

Use a graduated plastic transfer pipette to measure out the buttercream cupcake flour and stir this into the balm mixture. Scoop a pinch of matte purple pigment powder and one of lip-safe diamond dust mica and add them into the balm. You can adjust the amounts based on the shimmer and color you desire then stir to mix.

Fill lip balm pots with lip balm mixture using the plastic pipette. You can try using seven 1/3 ounce balm pots each holding about two ounces of lip balm. Reheat the lip balm in case it solidifies and continue to fill the containers. Put the lip balm into the fridge to facilitate hardening. Once hardened, you can decorate using Japanese Washi tape to make a cute gift without much strain.

Mint Lime Foot Soak

What you'll need

- Ribbon & paper embellishments
- 4 clean glass jars with lids
- 1-2 drops green food coloring
- 2-3 drops lime essential oil
- 2-3 drops peppermint essential oil
- Zest from 1 lime
- 2 cups Epsom salts

How to make

Combine peppermint essential oil, zest from one lime, green food coloring, lime essential oil and Epsom salts in a medium bowl. Mix to attain a light green mixture, and to distribute lime zest completely. Decant the mixture into jars and add decorations as desired.

To use the lime foot soak, sprinkle it into a foot spa appliance or into a dish pan dedicated for feet and fill this with warm water. Allow the feet to soak for a few hours as you read a book or watch TV.

Anti-Wrinkle Cream

What you'll need

- 2 egg whites
- ¼ pear
- 3 seedless grapes
- 1 tablespoon rosemary leaves

- 2 tablespoons buttermilk
- 1 teaspoon lime juice
- 1 teaspoon lemon juice
- 1 teaspoon apple juice

How to make

Put all the above ingredients into a blender and then process for 30 seconds on medium speed.

Once done, put the cream mixture into small jars. Decorate your jars and place a card on top with directions for use: *Dab the cream on wrinkles. Allow to dry and then rinse your face with warm water. The cream should be used within four days.*

Chapter 2: Home Décor Gift Ideas

Birch Bark Candles

What you'll need

- Leather string
- Large elastic
- Birch bark strips
- Large candles, especially battery operated
- Glue gun, optional

How to Make

Start by wrapping the elastic around your candle loosely. Tuck the bark inside so that it overlaps and covers your candle. Now cut it even with the height of your candle.

Add more pieces of the elastic to fully cover the candle, and then wrap a leather string around it a number of times. Then knot and trim the ends. If pieces appear to be sticking out, use some glue and press the elastic in place. Now remove the elastic.

Kitchen Tablet Holder

What you'll need

- Scrabble tile holder
- Child's building block
- Cutting board
- Wood glue

How to Make

Attach the scrabble tile holder unto the bottom front of your cutting board using wood glue then glue the building block at the back of your design.

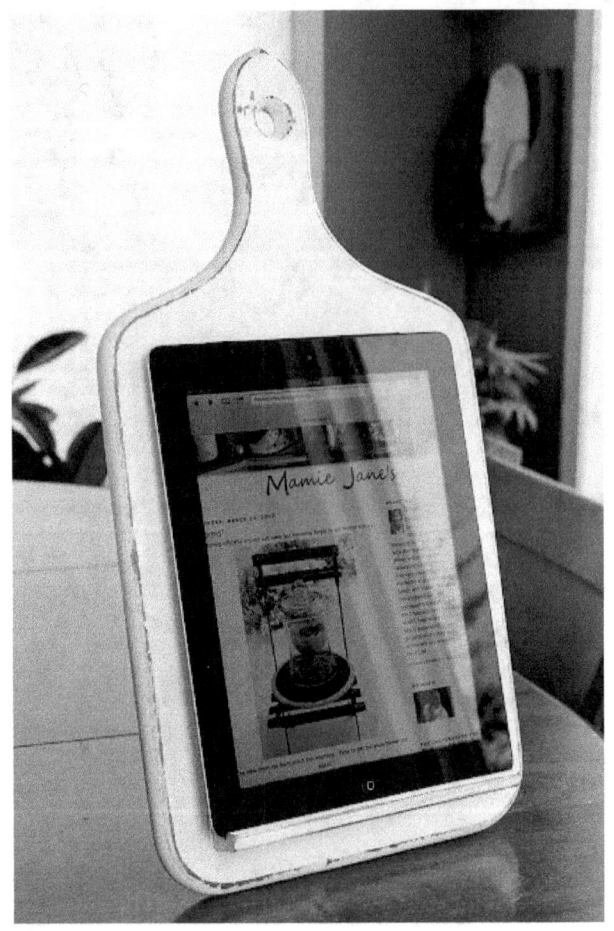

Allow the glue to dry and then apply paint. You can paint the holder white, sand the edges and then stain the piece to complete the look.

Mother's Day Printable

What you'll need

- 2×12" piece of pine wood
- Scissors

- Free printable
- Furniture nails
- A hammer

How to make

Get a 2×12" piece of pinewood to make a board that is 15 inches long. Stain this board with your preferred choice of paint. As the wood board dries, get your printable and cut it out using pair of scissors.

To rough the edges a bit, use a sander and then use furniture nails to add to your printable. Press the furniture nails with your hand or a hammer in order to fix it in place.

To the back of each clip, apply some drops of glue and then attach them to the board, then wait for it to dry and then add a few pictures for your mom, preferably 3×5 prints. If you want to have the gift hung on a wall, you can add a saw-tooth hanger at the back.

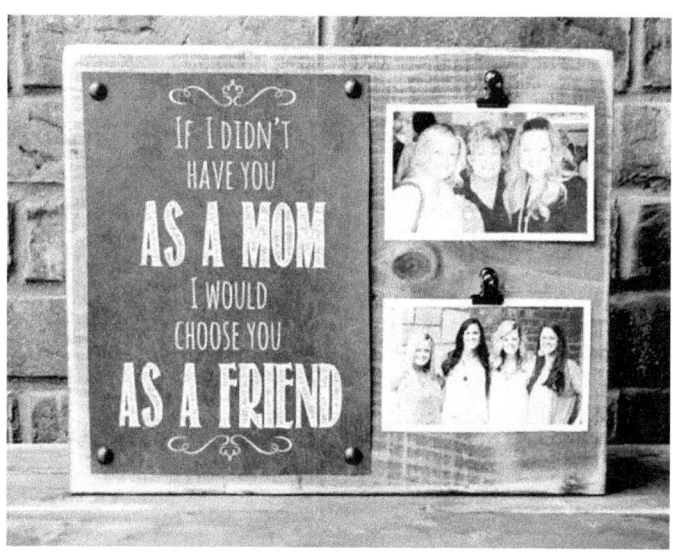

Tissue Paper Picture Frame

What you'll need

- Scissors
- Nail file block
- Mod Podge®
- Tissue paper
- Small wood frame

How to make

Determine your frame size and then cut a piece of a tissue paper to fit. A tissue paper is useful in giving your frame a wrinkly-shabby chic appearance.

In a photo editing software such as Photoshop, open a digital paper and resize it to 8.5 x 11. Send the file to your printer for normal printing.

Place the tissue paper in the paper feeder and then press the start button. If you experience problems in printing on the tissue paper, tape the tissue to a cardstock or regular paper.

Use Mod Podge® to coat the frame and then smooth out the air bubbles. Now cut an X mark gently through the middle of the frame.

Add some glue to the inside of your frame and then gently pull the loose edges of the tissue through the center. Press into the glue, and then allow some time to dry. When dry, trim away the excess tissue paper very carefully.

Allow the frame to dry for one more hour before smoothing the edges of your frame. To smooth, you can use sandpaper or the soft nail file and in the process remove any excess tissue paper.

Use Modge Podge® to coat more layers and allow to dry. You may choose to add other accessories after drying, such as fabric flowers, plastic toys or wooden letters.

Family Tree Serving Tray

What you'll need

- 6 labels
- A corn
- 4 leaves
- Leafless - bare tree
- House of 3 banners
- Mod Podge®

How to make

Obtain a funky tray; paint the border Valspar's Dreamy Clouds and paint the middle white. Obtain a number of leaves and get ready to glue them all down. A curvy tray is important in defining the fullness of your tree.

Stenciled Tea Towels

What you'll need

- Spray adhesive for stencils, repositionable

- Work surface; cardboard or white foam board

- Tea towels, washed and ironed
- Foam pouncers
- FolkArt® fabric painting medium
- FolkArt® acrylic paints in a variety of colors
- FolkArt® laser cut stencil

How to make

Lay a towel on a disposable work surface (since paint is likely to leak through the towel). Mix the acrylic paint based on the directions for the fabric medium. For instance, I mixed 4 teaspoons of acrylic paint with 2 teaspoons of fabric medium for each towel.

Use the repositionable spray adhesive to spray on the back of the stencil. Put it onto the tea towel and then smooth your fabric.

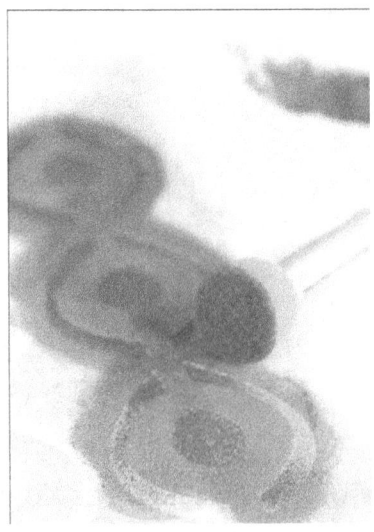

Load a pouncer using the mixture of paint and fabric medium and offload excess paint onto a paper before you apply on the tea towel. Fill the stencil through an up-and-down pouncing motion while you load and offload more paint as needed. Be careful not to push the sponge too hard to prevent the paint from seeping under the edges of your stencil.

After the stencil is filled in completely, remove it from the fabric and wash using water and soap. Wash every time to prevent paint smears as you move the stencil to a different section.

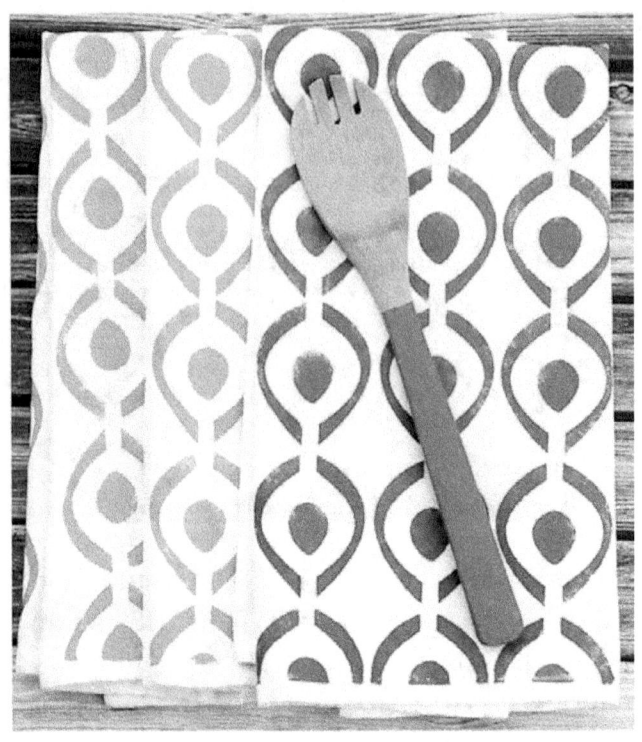

Now return the stencil to the towel to match with the established pattern. Once finished, allow your fabric to dry for about 1-2 days. Once dry, heat with an iron at low heat for 30 seconds to set and then machine wash on gentle cycle before you hang to dry.

Chapter 3:
Jewelry Gift Ideas

T-Shirt Necklace

What you'll need

- T-shirt
- Beads
- Hot glue
- Thick needle
- *How to Make*

Obtain a T-shirt, and cut it into strips.

To pull the strips through the beads, use a thick needle. Use about 2-3 beads for every strip of the T-shirt.

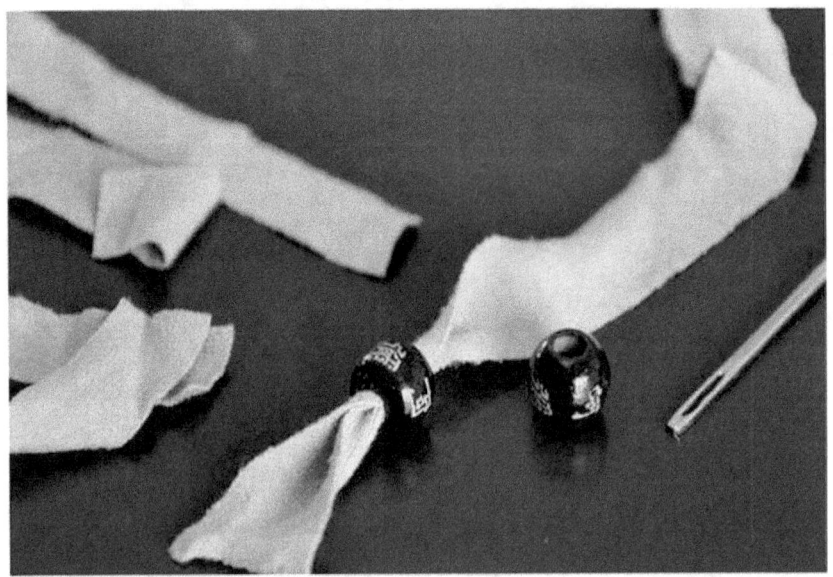

Make a few knots and ensure they are in place. Try to make them vary in position along the strips. To make the strips lengthen and roll up, pull them gently and then join the ends all up. Sew the threads together.

Now sew the other set of threads inwards to make them shorter. The shorter part will form the back of the necklace.

To make the design quite pretty, get the four strips left over from the previous trimming of the back part of the necklace. Wrap two of the strips around each of them, and hot-glue them into position.

Embossed Painted Can Flower

You can easily make this flower pendant just from an aluminum can and a copper rivet to join the 3 layers.

What you'll need

- Aluminum can
- Copper rivet
- Acrylic paint

How to Make

Obtain an aluminum can, rinse it and then cut it to make a sheet that can fit a die. Design and cut two flower shapes and a circle.

Now emboss the flower shapes and use a hammer to make the circle into a dome. If you don't want the original colors found on the can, use acrylic paint to paint the petals of the flower.

Allow to dry out, and then use an eyelet or a rivet to join the different layers. To make a jump ring, just punch a hole in the back of the flower petal. To complete the design, add a favorite cord or chain.

Bird Nest Necklace

What you'll need

- Jump ring and a clasp
- Necklace chain
- Pearls or glass beads
- Jewelry wire, gauge 20 or 24

How to Make

Get some nice beads, string them onto the wire and arrange them as you like, and then wrap the wire around them. Wrap some wire in the space between each bead to make 2-3 loops.

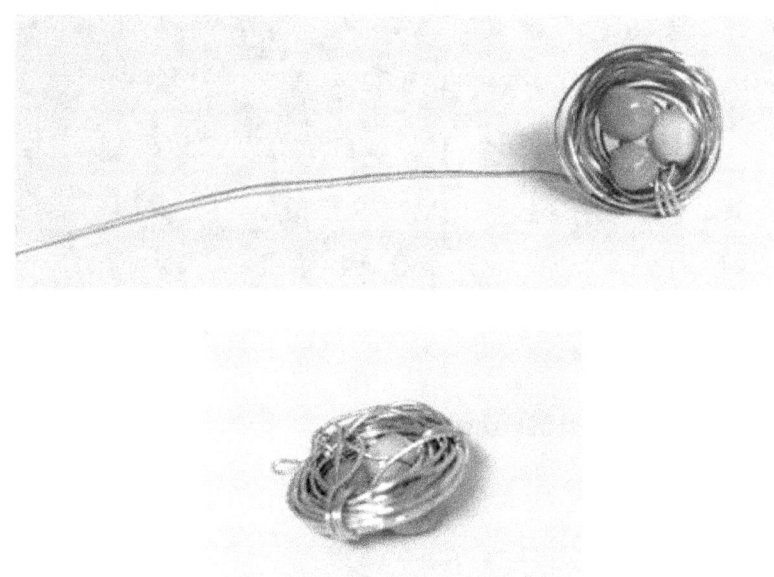

Now attach a jump ring and a clasp to the end of your necklace chain to complete your design.

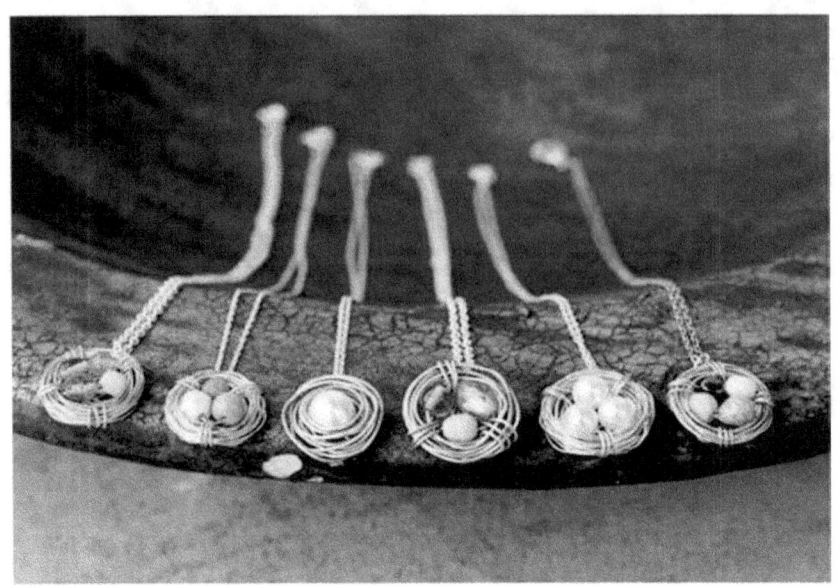

Painted Wooden Bracelets

What you need

- Paper plate
- Masking tape or Washi
- Cotton swabs
- Craft paint, 4 colors
- Wooden bracelets, various sizes

How to make

To make multicolored strips, obtain a masking tape or Washi to section off the bracelet as you like. Start painting various sections of your wooden bracelet using a paint brush over the tape edges. This helps in creating a clean line. Allow to dry before removing the tape.

To make multicolored finger prints, position a little dollop of about 4 colors of paint on a sheet of waxed paper or a paper plate. Choose the first color, dip into the paint and then randomly stamp on the external side of your bracelet. Redo the procedure to paint the bracelets on other colors.

To add more fingerprints, use your second color and fill it between your first color. Repeat the operation with the third and fourth colors. Overlap the fingerprints so as to design a unique effect.

You can also make pint-sized polka dots using a cotton swab for each paint color.

Button Necklace

What you'll need

- Chain or ribbon

- Clasp
- 2 jump rings
- 2 crimp beads
- Tiger-tail wire
- Variety of buttons

How to make

Gather all the materials, including the buttons. Using a wire cutter, cut out a piece of wire to fit the button portion of the necklace. Add about 4 inches allowance to this wire.

Next, put a crimp head and a jump ring into the wire, and then loop it back through the crimp head. You should tightly pull it as you squish the bead using jewelry pliers.

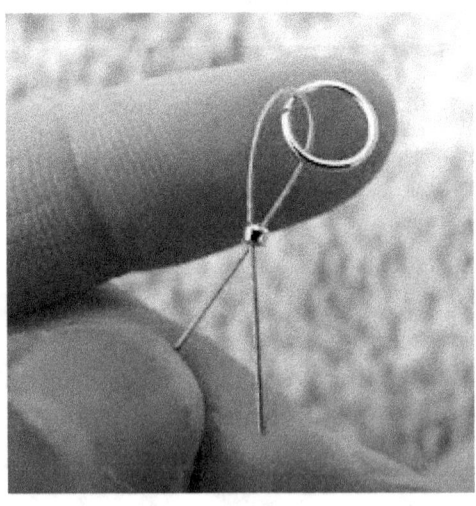

Put your beads onto the wire, starting with the wooden beads.

Then string the buttons along your wire, until you have about 2 inches of wire left. To complete the design, end with the beads.

To the wire, add a jump ring and a crimp head and then loop the wire back through the crimp bead. Pull the loop tightly, thread the unnecessary wire just down through your wooden beads, and then smash the crimp bead.

If your beads have big openings that could make the crimp head slip into the hole, just add a smaller bead at the end as you include the crimp head. Complete your necklace by adding in a chain or a ribbon to the jump ring then clasp at the back.

DIY Thumbprint Necklace

What you'll need

- Pliers

- Necklace
- Circular template
- Jump ring
- Pen
- Wax paper
- Bake-able clay

How to make

1. Preheat your oven to 275° F and then put wax paper on the bottom and top of a clay ball. Roll out the clay ball to flatten, ensuring that you do not roll it too thin, and then punch out a pendant from your circular template.

Mark out a hole for the jump ring at the top of the pendant and cut it out. Then press a thumbprint of a child, applying some pressure to get the best imprint. Place the pendant into the oven and bake for around 15 minutes per inch or according to the instructions for the clay you're using.

Remove from your oven and chill for a few hours. If required, you can spray with clear enamel to assist in preserving and add the shine.

Fix a jump ring through the hole and then close it and string the necklace through it.

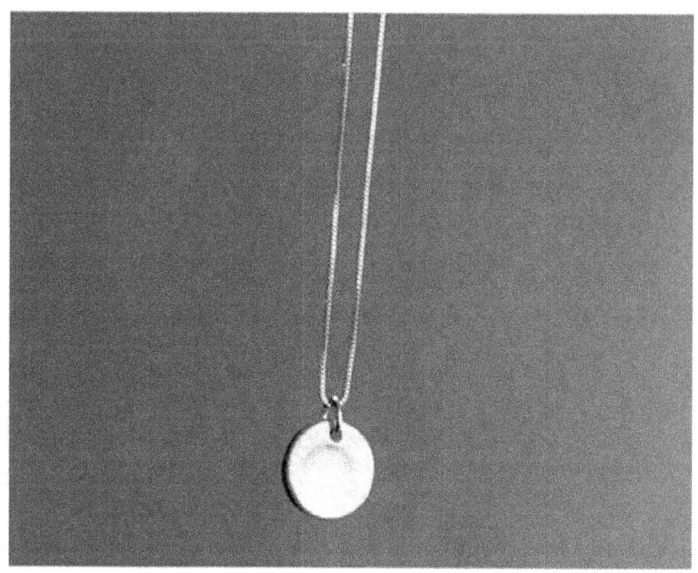

In case you don't have the actual raw material, try improvising some of the required items. For instance, you can make large holes to run the leather coding or ribbon in case you don't have jump rings. You can also make pendants from salt dough and spray with metallic spray paint to make it look like silver or gold. Spray with clear enamel in order to preserve and make it shinier. To make a template, use a circle punch or anything that is circular.

Mother's Day Succulent Rings

What you'll need

- Scissors or small clippers
- Succulents with smaller foliage
- Reindeer moss
- Floral cold glue

- Small pliers

- Wire-cutters

- 12-gauge Oasis aluminum wire

How to make

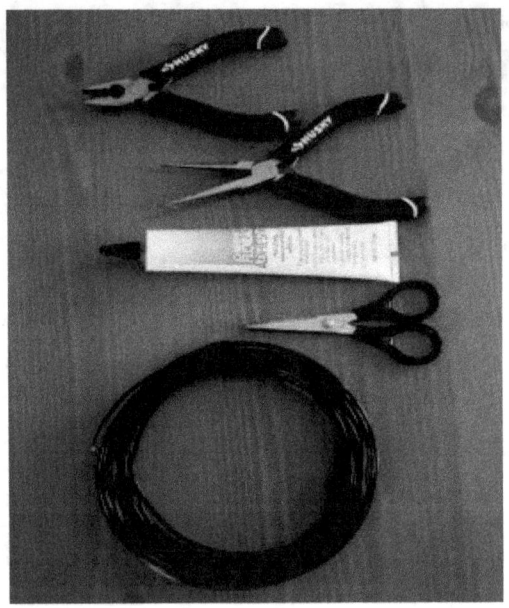

Obtain 8-inch long pieces of floral aluminum wire, place your ring finger in the middle of this wire and then bend the wire around your finger. Leave two long ends.

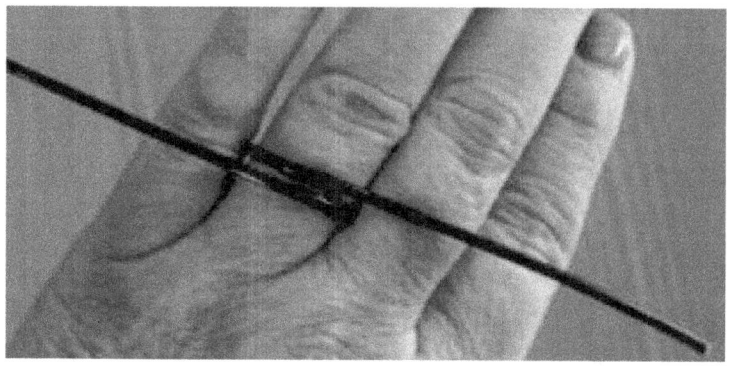

Make an L shape by bending each wire and then spiral each end toward the ring base. In doing this, make an armature to hold the succulents in place.

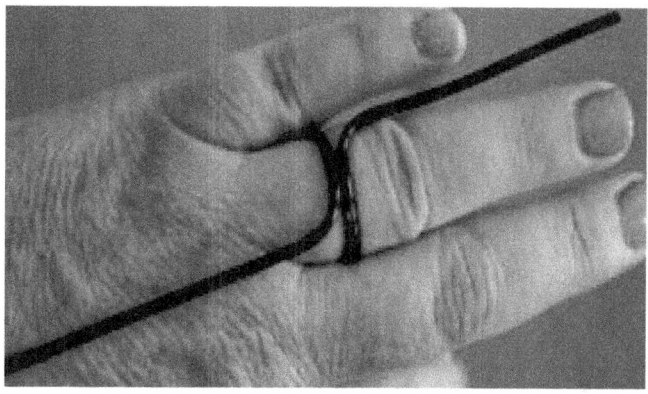

Take out the ring from the finger and then attach moss or a leaf to the armature using glue. Allow a few minutes to dry before you trim the moss to match the shape of your ring.

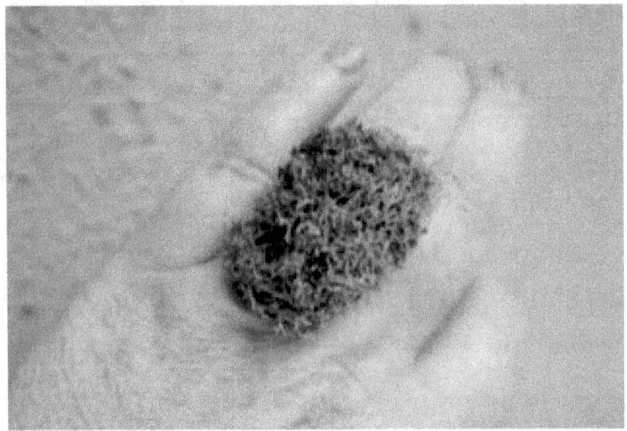

Now attach the succulents to the leaf or moss, starting with the larger pieces. Give time for the pieces to dry and then attach more of them to get the desired design.

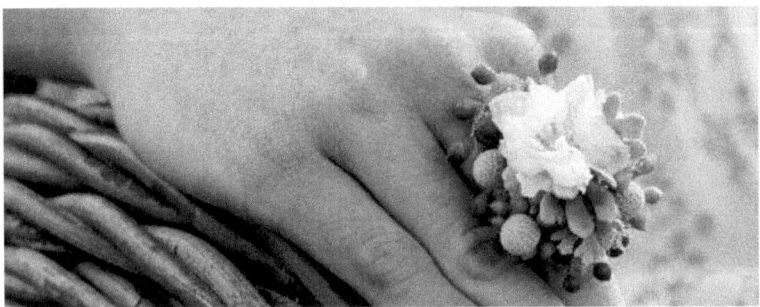

Chapter 4:
Clothes and Accessories Gift Ideas

Leather Tassels

What you'll need

- Piece of leather
- Fabric rolling cutter
- Ruler and pen

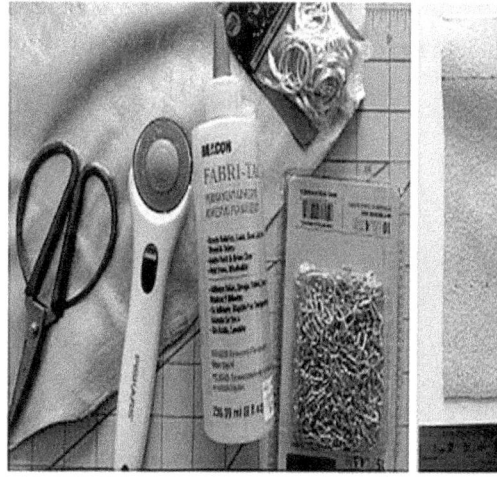 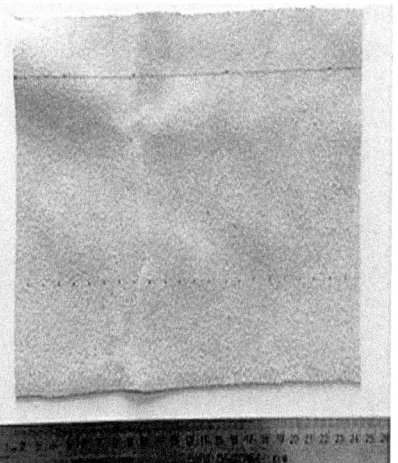

How to Make

Start by cutting a section of your leather, about 9 inches wide.

Mark a top section on the back side of the leather and then mark vertical marks for the tassels. You can use a ruler and a pen to measure and mark the leather.

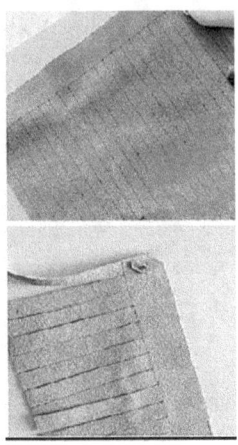

Use a pair of scissors or a fabric rolling cutter to cut the leather. Then position the chain inside the leather material, run a line of Fabri-Tac® glue through the tassel and then roll it up.

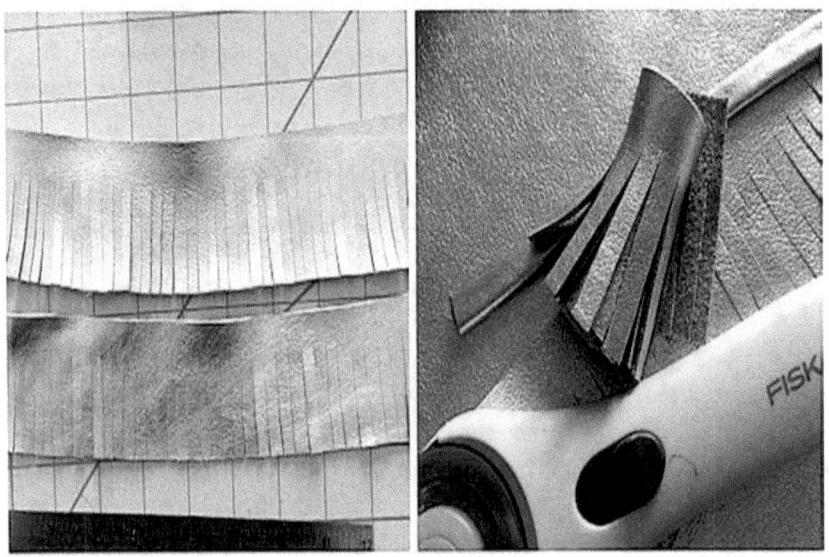

Put a rubber band around the ends or hold them shut using your finger until the tassels dry. When done, just attach the chain to a key chain ring.

Doily Canvas Bag

What you'll need

- Paper finishes adhesive spray
- Paper doily
- Fabric paint
- Canvas bag

How to make

Spray the doily with some paper spray adhesive then press down the adhesive on the bag. Now paint gently over the holes using fabric paint, which is more durable than crafts paint.

Before the paint dries out, just pull back your doily. In case it tears, carefully peel off its pieces.

Trace on your letter and fill it using paint. To complete and set it, do some ironing on the bag.

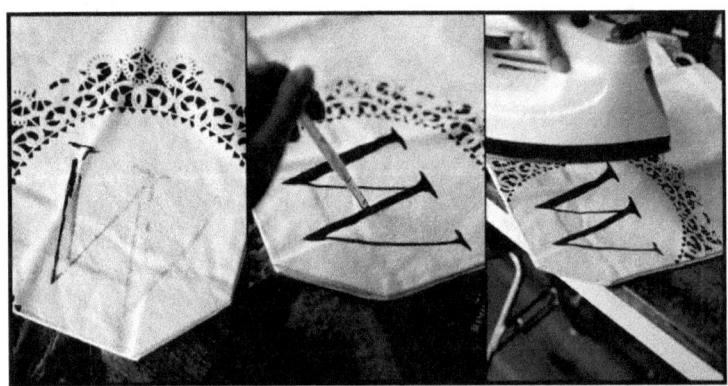

DIY Shoe Clips

What you'll need

- Toothpick
- Pliers
- E6000® craft adhesive
- A pair of blank shoe clips
- A pair of vintage costume earrings

How to make

Wiggle the ear clip hinge back and forth from the base with the help of pliers. Open a blank shoe clip then apply glue on the outer and flat surface.

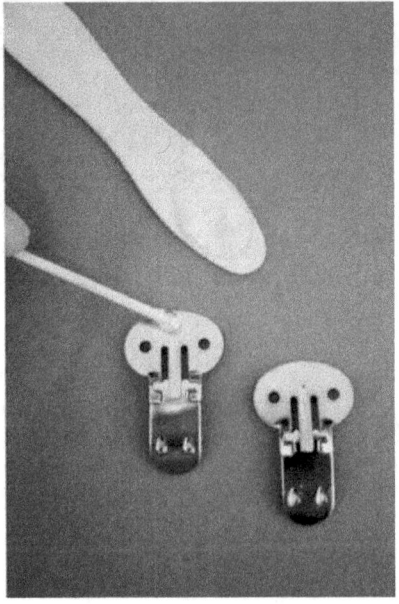

Now press the blank shoe clip against the back side of the earring, making sure the area where the shoe clip is to be joined is bigger than the shoe clip. Redo the procedure for the other earring. Let it dry for a few hours.

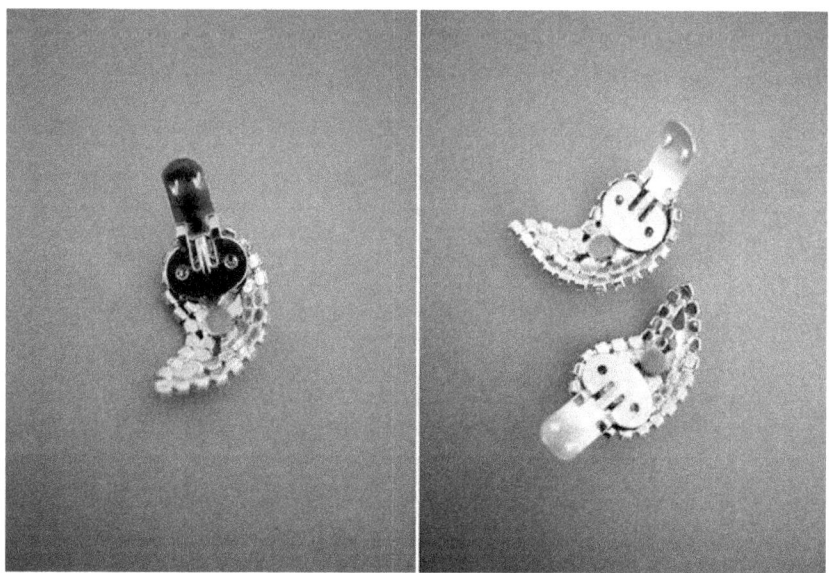

The shoe clips should have two small metal prongs that are joined to the underside of the shoes. This helps to keep the clip firmly fastened. The top of the clip should also be smooth to prevent damaging the shoes.

To the blank area of the shoe clip, apply a sufficient amount of glue and then press it against the back side of the earring. Repeat the step again and allow it to dry. Finally, clip the fully done clip onto a pair of flats.

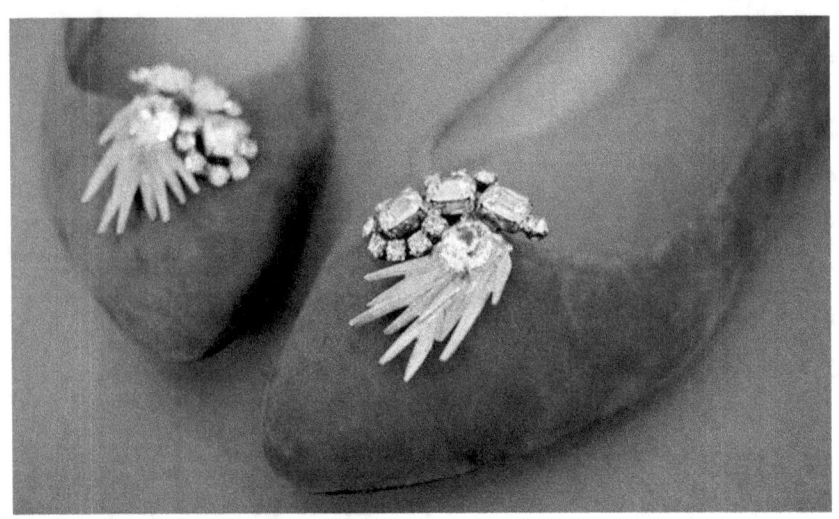

An-Hour Bag Gift

What you'll need

- 2 large buttons
- 1 strip of wadding about 2 1/2 x 29 inches
- 2 strips of fabric 3 x 29 inches for the strap
- 2 x 6 ½ inch squares fabric for the pocket
- 2 pieces for wadding or batting
- 2 pieces for your handbag fabric
- 1 magnetic purse snap, optional
- 2 pieces for your lining fabric

How to make

Start your gift bag from the pocket. Put the right sides of your squares together and then sew around, leaving about ¼ inch allowance from the edge. Also, leave about 3 inches gap for turning and then snip off the corners. Ensure you do not cut your stitching.

Through the gap, turn the right sides out and iron the fabric if desired. You can also do a line of stitching across the place to become the top of the pocket.

Now pin the pocket to the right side of the lining of your bag. Then sew around the sides and bottom of the pocket ensuring that you catch the gap you had. This will be for turning in your stitching.

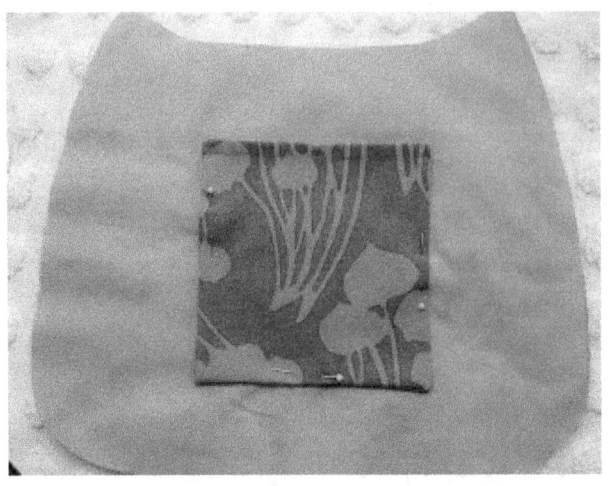

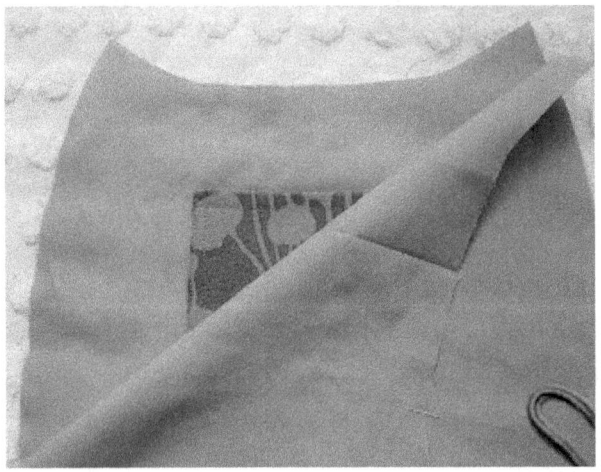

You can sew two lines in order to improve the appearance as well as to strengthen your design. Then put the other lining piece with the right sides together with the pocketed one. Sew around the bag, and leave a turning gap at the bottom.

Hold your bag fabric pieces. Now affix your batting or wadding to the wrong side of every piece then sew all the 4 pieces simultaneously. Ensure that the right sides of your fabric are aligned together with the wadding on the outer of each. You can try pinning in order to stop the pieces from moving.

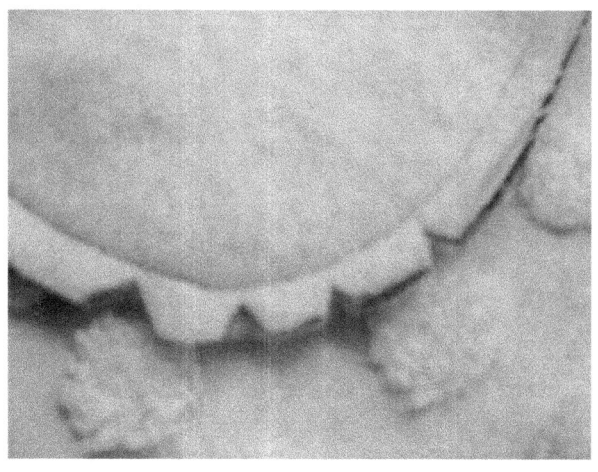

After this, sew around the sides as well as the base of your bag using a ¼ inch seam. To make your curves quite smooth, you may try clipping them. Now turn your bag right side out. Slip the bag into your lining. You should now have the right sides of the lining of the pocket against the right sides of your bag.

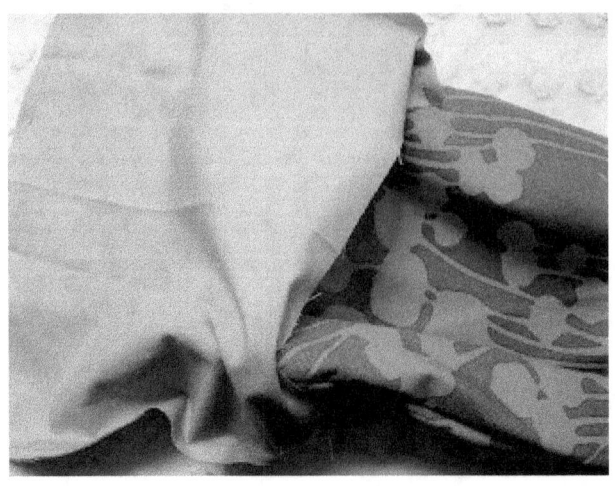

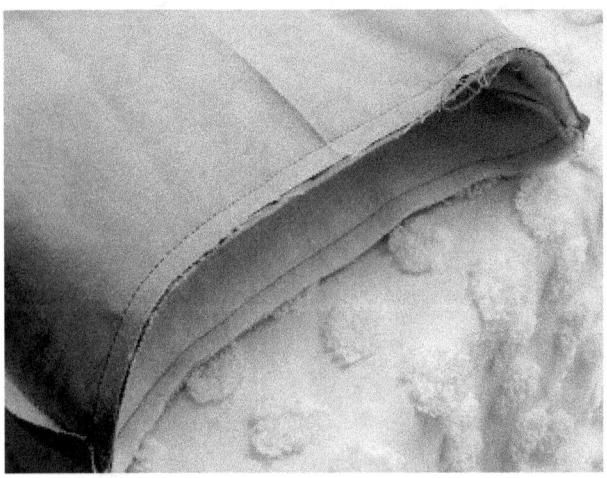

Sew around the top opening of your bag then turn your entire bag right side out through the gap occurring at the bottom of the lining. Turn this lining inside the bag, and smooth it all the way and then pin around the top and do topstitch.

If you need to add a magnetic snap, put your hand into the bag through the lining gap, and then poke your snaps through and then affix them. You may choose to use a wadding reinforced with an interfacing or put a small circle of cardboard on the inside.

Close the gap of the lining closed by hand or machine sewing. Start designing your strap. Put the right sides of your pieces together and then sew them along the entire length of the strips on the two sides. If you like, you may add your wadding and then sew it in.

From here, turn the right sides out in order to form a long tube. Thread in a long strip of the wadding body using a safety pin. Tuck in your ends, either straight across or at an angle and then top stitch all around. As you do this, ensure that you catch the ends of the fabric into your sewing.

Finally, attach the strap into the bag through a machine or hand stitching technique, and then include a number of buttons to decorate your bag. For this, you can try out a patchwork of fabric together before adding some trims.

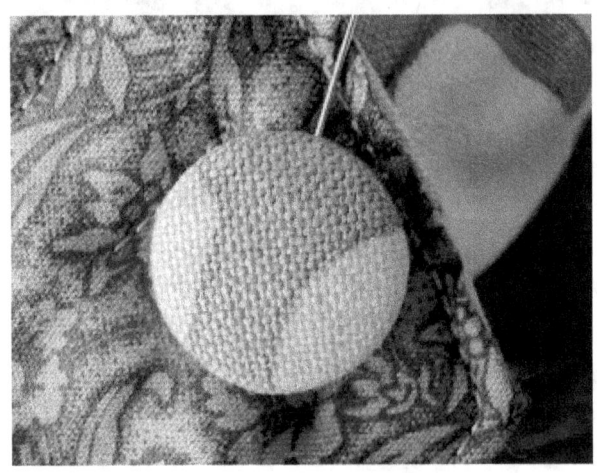

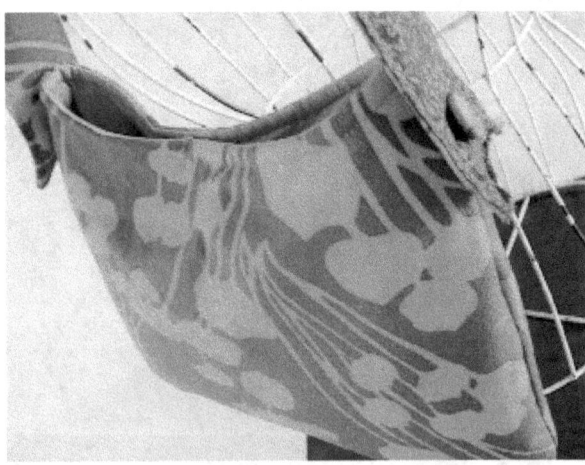

Super Easy Summer Dress

What you'll need

- Fabric, about 2 yards
- Sewing machine

How to make

Start by cutting a big square of fabric, such as stretchy jersey cotton. Make the cutting about 6 inches longer than the actual measurement, from the floor to your bust. Also, leave the fabric longer wide than your actual measurement around for the gather.

Sew your fabric into a kind of a tube as shown here.

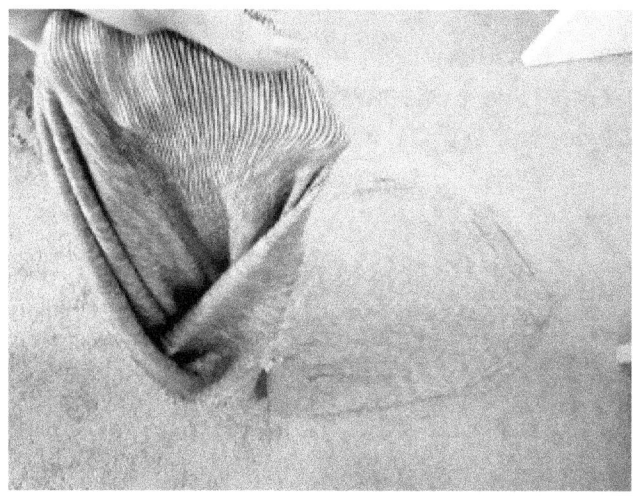

Next, sew a hem around the top, making it wider to allow elasticity. Leave a small opening to use to slide your elastic in. Position a safety pin on the end of your elastic. Now slide it the entire way around the dress, before sewing the elastic closed.

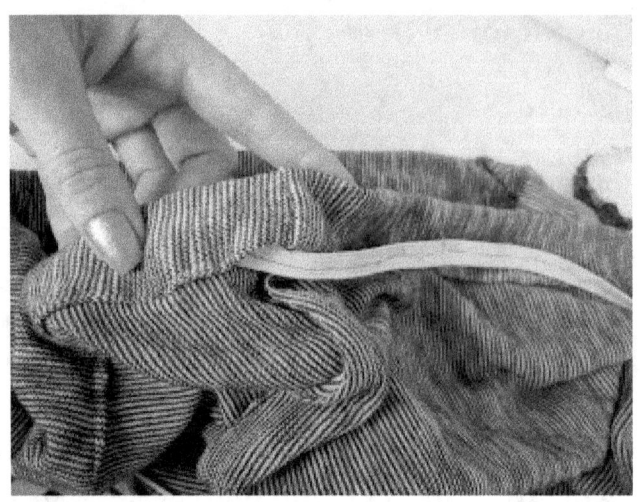

Obtain three long strips of material in a coordinating or matching color and then knot them together at one of the end. Then braid the entire fabric pieces and then knot the other end.

Now measure out the length of your dress and trim as desired. You may hem it or just leave it, especially if its jersey cotton fabric that doesn't fray. You can design the dress by knotting the braided tie around the waist or just twist it up to be tied around the neck.

Infinity Scarf

What you'll need

- 1 yard of fabric (or 1.5 yards)
- Sewing machine

How to make

Start by making a long fabric tube by folding the fabric in half to get the longest length possible. Then cut down the middle of the fold to obtain two long strips.

Then straight stitch the long strips together at one of the ends, with the right sides of the fabric facing together.

Now fold down the ends of the fabric and straight stitch across to make two finished ends. Fold the fabric in half a second time, the inside facing out, to get a thinner strip. Then straight stitch down the open side to finish the fabric tube.

Turn the fabric to have the right side out, and stitch up the two ends of the fabric tube to make a circle. You can then make two loops with the scalp when you wear it. If you have a longer fabric, make the scarf with three loops to make it full size.

Add Beaded Fringe to Pants

What you'll need

- Scissors
- Pony beads
- A pair of jeans or khakis

How to make

Cut the hem off the bottom of your pant leg, and then cut thin strips about 6 inches up the pant legs. You can make the strips longer to fit more pony beads.

Then thread your beads. Just slip 2-3 pony beads on every strip, ensuring that you have sufficient length for tying a knot.

Once done, tie the end of the strip into a knot. Use a double knot to make it more secure.

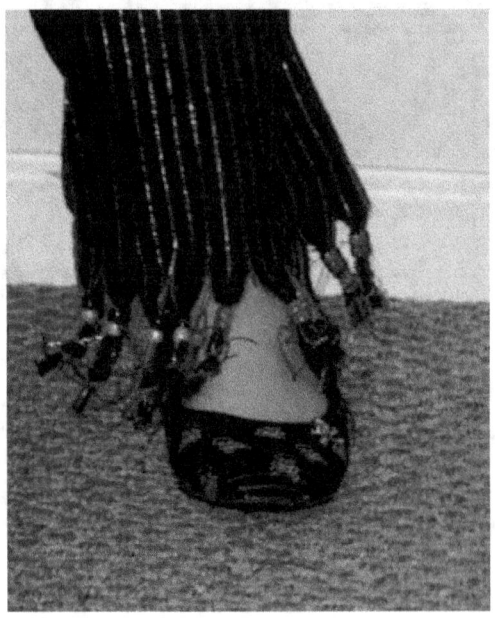

Chapter 5: Food Gift Ideas

Iced Chai Tea Latte Mix

What you'll need

- 1 teaspoon ground cloves
- 1 teaspoon allspice
- 2 teaspoons ground cinnamon
- 2 teaspoons ground ginger
- 1½ cups instant tea, unsweetened
- 2½ cups white sugar
- 1 cup French vanilla flavored creamer, non-dairy
- 1 cup powdered creamer, non-dairy
- 1 cup dry milk powder, nonfat

How to make

Put the above ingredients in a food processor and process until they turn into fine powder. Then pour into several small jars or one large jar to make 36 servings of iced chai tea latte mix. You can use the mix for cold or hot drinks.

Prepare the packaging for the tea latte mix, using cute jars and little spoons and ribbon to decorate the gift.

To prepare hot drinks, add 2 heaping tablespoons of the mix to a cup of water, or add to milk or water for cold drinks and then stir well.

Gift Box Cookies

What you'll need

- Decorating icing
- 2 cups all-purpose flour
- ½ teaspoon baking powder
- ¼ teaspoon salt
- 1½ teaspoons vanilla extract
- 1 large egg
- ½ cup each confectioner's and granulated sugar
- 1 stick unsalted butter, softened
- Disposable pastry bags, fitted with 1⁄8-inch plain tip
- Sugar pearls or blue dragées
- 2 ¾-inch gift box cutter

How to make

Into a mixer over low speed, beat the sugars and butter until fluffy. Then beat in the baking powder, vanilla, egg and salt. Now add in floor and continue to beat until fully blended.

Sub-divide your dough into two portions, and then shape each of them into an inch thick disk. Wrap it separately in plastic and then chill until firm, for an hour or so. Meanwhile, preheat the oven to 350° F.

Obtain re-usable non-stick liners, non-stick foil or parchment paper and line your baking sheet. Roll out the remaining disk of dough on a flat surface to a scant ¼ inch thickness. Then cut out about 12 pieces dough scraps using a floured 2¾-inch gift box cutter.

Transfer the cut circles into the prepared baking sheets using a floored spatula. Lay the dough about 2 inches apart and then bake into the oven for about 11-13 minutes, until your cookies' edges turn golden. Remove from oven and cool the cookies on sheet on a wire rack for some time. Transfer to the rack to now cool completely.

Obtain and fill a pastry bag fitted with a #5 writing tip with thick white icing. Pipe outline onto your cookies in order to make a 3-dimentional box that has a bow on top. Place a dragée at the center of the bow while the icing is still wet. Allow the cookie to dry fully, within 4-6 hours.

Icing Sugar

In a large bowl, beat 3¼ cups of confectioners' sugar together with a ¼ cup of Just Whites. Beat with a mixer that is on low speed until fully combined. Add in about 1/3 cup water and continue to beat until fully blended. Then increase the speed to high, and beat for 8 additional minutes, until the icing turns white and thick. You'll make 2½ cups.

Peach Strawberry Butterfly Cake

What you'll need

- 1 tablespoon sugar
- 1 cup diced, peeled peach
- 1½ cups strawberries, hulled, cut lengthwise in wedges
- 1 cup heavy cream, whipping
- 1 box, (3 ounce) peach gelatin
- 1 frozen pound cake (10.75 ounce), thawed

How to make

Obtain a pastry bag that is fitted with a large star tip together with a 2¼ inch round metal cookie cutter. Now line 12 regular muffin cups using foil liners.

Cut 4 circles using a cookie cutter from the top to the bottom of your cake. Ensure each cut piece has 6 rounds. Put one in the bottom of each lined cup, and then set aside the other 12 that remain of the initial 24.

Add about ¾ cup of boiling water to gelatin in a medium bowl. Stir until fully dissolved. Refrigerate and continue to regularly stir every 25 minutes. You should have a thick consistency of unbeaten egg whites.

On medium-high speed beat about ½ cup of cream in a mixer until soft peaks form after you lift the beaters. Stir a large spoonful into the peach mixture and then fold in the rest of the cream. Now fold in the peach and strawberries.

Without wasting time, just spoon into the lined cups and then top using the reserved pound cake rounds. Tightly cover the pan using a plastic wrap and then refrigerate for more than 3 hours to firm up the cake.

When serving, just remove the liners and then cut your cakes into half. On a plate, position the two cake halves with the round sides touching. In a small bowl, beat the rest of the sugar and cream with a mixer to form stiff peaks after beaters are lifted. When ready, spoon it into a pastry bag and then pipe a line down the center.

Butterfingers Dip

What you'll need

- 10 ounces marshmallow cream
- 8 ounces cream cheese
- 10 fun size butterfingers

How to make

Into a bowl, combine marshmallow cream and soft cream cheese together.

Chop about 10 butterfingers in bite-size pieces and then add into the cream mixture. Also chop 2 butterfingers and then sprinkle onto the topping.

Crêpes with Strawberries and Muscat-Yogurt Sauce

What you'll need

- Confectioners' sugar, for dusting
- 24 strawberries, sliced
- ¼ teaspoon grated orange zest
- 1 tablespoon Muscat dessert wine
- 2 tablespoons honey
- 1 cup plain low-fat yogurt

- Vegetable oil

- 1 large egg

- ¾ cup skim milk

- ½ teaspoon salt

- ½ cup all-purpose flour

How to make

Whisk together salt and flour in a small bowl and then add in a tablespoon of oil together with the egg and milk. Continue to whisk until smooth. Allow the mixture to rest for around 20 minutes, covered. Whisk yogurt, zest, Muscat and honey in a separate bowl.

Preheat your oven to 350° F as you heat an 8-inch non-stick skillet. Use an oiled paper towel to rub the pan and then add in about 3 tablespoons of crème batter. Swirl the pan to coat, pouring off the excess batter.

Over moderate heat, cook the crepe for about 2 minutes, until the bottom has brown spots and the sides turn crisp. Now flip the crepe and allow to cook for 1 more minute. Then transfer it to the baking sheet and repeat the procedure to make 7 more crepes.

Once done with the 8 crepes, fold them into quarters and bake in the preheated oven for around 4 minutes.

To serve, put each of them onto a plate and then top with yogurt sauce. Use strawberries for garnish. Dust using the confectioners' sugar and then serve. The recipe makes one serving. This is an amazing recipe to prepare just for your mom to show her how much you love her.

Chocolate Brownie Cake

What you'll need

- 2 tablespoons cocoa powder
- ½ teaspoon baking powder
- 100g plain flour
- 1 teaspoon vanilla extract /essence
- 2 eggs
- 1 tablespoon golden syrup
- 125 g chocolate (plain or milk)
- 75 g light brown or muscovado sugar
- 175 g caster sugar
- 100 g butter

How to make

Preheat your oven to 180° F as you grease and line a 20 cm cake tin.

Into a pan, put golden syrup, chocolate, brown sugar, caster sugar, and butter and then melt gently on low heat to obtain a smooth and lump-free liquid.

Once melted, remove the pan from heat. Break the eggs into a separate bowl and whisk with a fork to obtain a light and frothy substance.

To the chocolate mixture, add in cocoa powder, baking powder, flour, vanilla extract or essence and eggs and combine fully.

Place the mixture into the greased cake tin and put it on the middle shelf of your oven. Now bake for around 25-30 minutes.

Remove from heat, chill for around 20-30 minutes and then cut into wedges and serve. The cake can be served with ice cream or cream and plenty of flesh fruit.

What an amazing way to treat your mom!

Granola with Lots of Dried Fruit

What you'll need

- ½ cup dried fruit, minced
- 1 tablespoon vegetable oil, e.g. safflower oil

- 2 tablespoons molasses
- 2 tablespoons honey
- ¼ teaspoon cardamom, ground
- ½ teaspoon cinnamon, ground
- 1 teaspoon kosher salt
- ¼ cup brown sugar
- 2 tablespoons pumpkin seeds, salted and roasted
- 2 tablespoons sunflower seeds, roasted
- 2 tablespoons agave nectar or granulated white sugar
- 1/3 cup wheat germ
- 1½ cups rolled oats

How to make

Preheat your oven to 250° F and combine all the dry ingredients in a mixing bowl, apart from the dried fruit. Use your hands to combine the ingredients.

Combine vegetable oil, molasses, and honey in a small bowl until fully combined. Add this mixture to the dry mixture, and use your hands to mix together. Ensure the ingredients are well coated into the honey and molasses mixture.

Spread the mixture evenly onto a baking sheet and bake for 30-35 minutes. Keep stirring the mixture after every 8-10 minutes as you pull the contents from the edges and corners of the pan into the middle of the baking sheet. Re-spread the mixture and rotate the cookie sheet after stirring. Bake until the mixture begins to darken a shade or two and you can sense the smell of spices from the mixture.

Take out of the oven and then fold in the dried fruit. Continue to fold to ensure the dried fruit is warmed by the mixture. Allow the granola and fruit to dry until crispy and then store in decorated jars.

Edible Flowers for Mother's Day

What you'll need

For the cupcakes:

- Natural food coloring

- 100 g natural yogurt

- 2 large eggs

- Fine salt

- 2 lemons

- 175 g caster sugar

- 225 g self-rising flour

- 175 g unsalted butter, melted and cooled a little

For the butter-cream icing:

- Fresh mint

- Poppy seeds

- For the garnish

- 125 g unsalted butter

- 250 g icing sugar

How to prepare

Start by preheating the oven to 350° F, or to 340° F if using a fan-assisted oven. Then line a 12-hole cupcake or muffin tin using paper cupcake cases.

Over a double boiler or in a pan, melt butter gently and then set aside to chill for some time. Meanwhile, in a large bowl, add self-rising flour and mix with a pinch of salt, lemon zest and sugar. Whisk together the ingredients to combine them.

Mix together butter, yogurt and the eggs in another bowl and whisk until smooth. Combine the dry and wet ingredients gently to obtain a lump-free batter. Add in adequate food coloring, keeping in mind that some color is lost during baking.

Sub-divide the batter into 12 cupcakes cases and then bake in the preheated oven for 20 minutes on the middle shelf. Insert a toothpick into the cupcakes to see if it comes out clean. If it doesn't, the cupcakes aren't ready and should be baked for some 2-5 more minutes. Once done, remove from heat and chill.

Prepare the butter cream icing by adding half of the icing sugar with the butter to a bowl and using an electric whisk to beat until smooth. Then add in lemon juice and the remaining icing sugar, continue to beat the mixture until smooth, and add your food coloring. Add more coloring to make the icing darker than the cupcakes, especially if using the same color for both the cakes and icing. This gives a two-tone contrast to the flowers. Beat the colored icing to obtain a fluffy mixture. Transfer the batter into a piping bag that is fitted with an open star nozzle.

It's time to assemble the cupcake flower. Using a sharp, serrated knife, cut the rounded top of every cupcake laid on its side. Ensure you leave a flat base to build upon. Slice the rounded top into fine slices that are 3 mm thick. Cut out flowers from the thin cupcake slices using a large 5-petal flower cutter meant for icing.

Now pipe a little amount of icing onto the flat top of each cupcake to cover it. Remove the flowers and then cut out each petal using a paring knife. Then overlay the petals around the edges of your pan cake to make a ring that goes all the way round the edge. Now tuck the last petal under the first one you laid down.

To complete the edible flowers, pipe a little flower into the center of the cupcake and use a small amount of poppy seeds to garnish. Remove a few of the little leaves at the center of a mint bunch, and place them to stick out from under your cake petals. Do this at regular intervals all around the edge of your cupcake.

Chapter 6: Other Gift Ideas

Fabric Covered Books

What you'll need

- Decorative ribbons and some glue
- Scissors
- Fabric tape
- Self-adhesive fabric
- Notebooks

How to Make

Note the length and width of your notebook, and then cut out two pieces of adhesive tape, a little bigger than the book. You need one for the front and the other for the back.

Take away the protective paper from the notebook and then put the fabric on top, with the sticky side facing downwards. Fold the corners first to get them looking pretty.

After folding the corners, fold along the sides and then cut the fabric tape to match the proper length. Then take away the backing paper and cover the spine. If desired, you can decorate the notebook along the spine, using an additional tape.

To finish decorating the book, use a small piece of fabric ribbon that has text such as "home-made", and then stick it at the back of the notebook. These books are suitable for note taking, recipes or diaries.

Fabric Scrap Key Chain

What you'll need

- Thread and other sewing stuff
- Buttons, felt, for embellishing
- Pinking shears
- Key ring
- Twill tape or grosgrain ribbon
- Small piece of Pellon® Peltex® one-sided iron-on interfacing
- Medium weight iron-on interfacing
- Fabric scraps
- Something to make your pattern with

How to Make

Select the scraps to use, and then iron them on the medium that interfaces the wrong side of your fabric. In case you would do buttons or an appliqué, first trace around the pattern onto the right side of the fabric. This should help you understand how to place it.

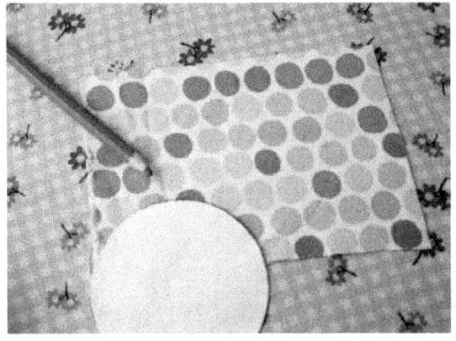

Add a quick appliquéd C to the fabric and then follow the directions to iron the Peltex® to the wrong side of your fabric. Iron the shiny side of the Peltex® on the wrong side of the fabric. Put it down, use a pressing cloth to cover and then press the iron on it for about 10-15 seconds. When ironing, do it to the side that forms the front of the keychain.

Cut the Peltex® out, just along the back side of your key chain. Now position the wrong side together, and then place the two pins about an inch on the bottom.

Now sew them together from pin to pin, just around the circle. Sew about ¼ inch from the edge. Using pinking shears, trim the edges all the way around to have this design:

Cut out a piece of your ribbon or twill tape about 2 inches long, and then fold it over the key ring. Then insert into the opening on the bottom of the key chain. Sew the opening to close it using back stitching from the beginning to end. To complete the design, trim the ends, and make more key chains.

Mother's Day Gardening Gift

What you'll need

- Ribbon
- Confetti or tissue paper
- Tape
- Skewers
- Seed packets
- Gardening tools/shovel
- Empty paint bucket

- Gloves

How to make

Obtain some skewers and tape them to the back of your seed packets. Use filler such as confetti to fill your bucket and then put the gardening tools and seeds packets inside. If desired, you can put a card on a stick to complete the gift. This is a perfect gift for a mom who adores gardening.

Mason Jar Sewing Kits

What you'll need

- Straight pins & other sewing notions

- Pen or pencil

- Scrapbook paper, matching your fabric scraps

- Hot glue/glue gun

- Fiber fill

- Pretty fabric

- Small Mason jars

How to make

On the wrong side of your scrapbook paper, trace the lid of the Mason jar to obtain circles to use inside each jar's lid.

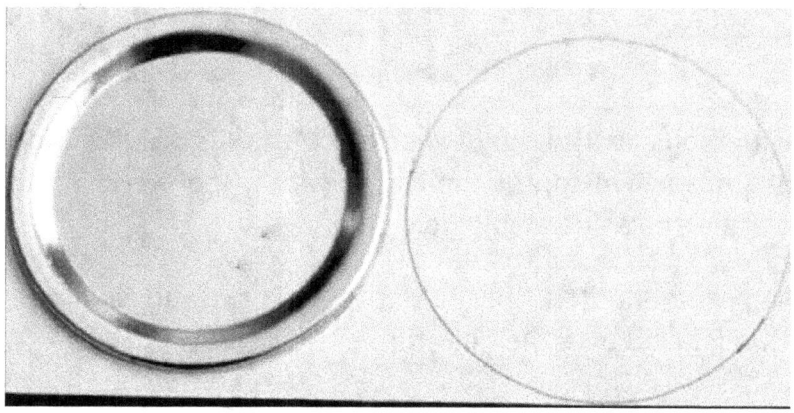

Now cut out a 4x4 piece of the fabric you'll be using.

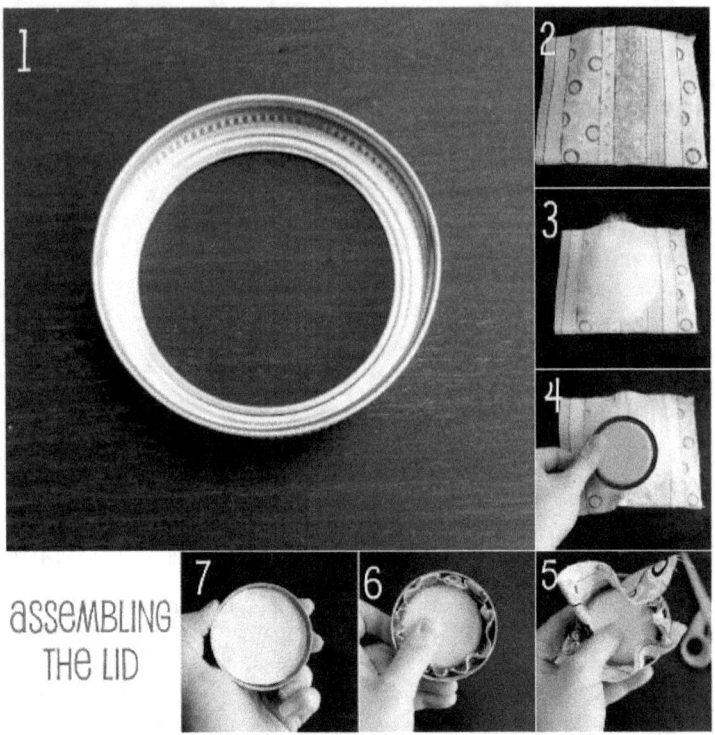

assembling the lid

To assemble, lay the rim of your lid on the surface, the top side facing down. On top of the rim, position the piece of fabric, with the wrong side facing up.

Now position a little fiber fill on your fabric, and then put the Mason jar's lid over the fiber fill.

Slightly push the fabric, the fiber fill and the lid through the Mason jar rim, making it pop a bit. You should have an allowance where you can poke straight pins into.

Get the lid securely inside the rim and then use scissors to trim away the excess fabric. Lay the fabric flat using your hot glue gun.

Using the scrapbook paper circle you initially cut out, just cover the insides of your lid s to conceal any jagged fabric edges or hot glue.

Threaded Washer Pendant

What you'll need

- Glue
- Scissors
- Thread
- Washers

How to make

Tie a thread onto a washer and wrap the washer completely with the thread a number of times. Wrap all the way around and then do it again.

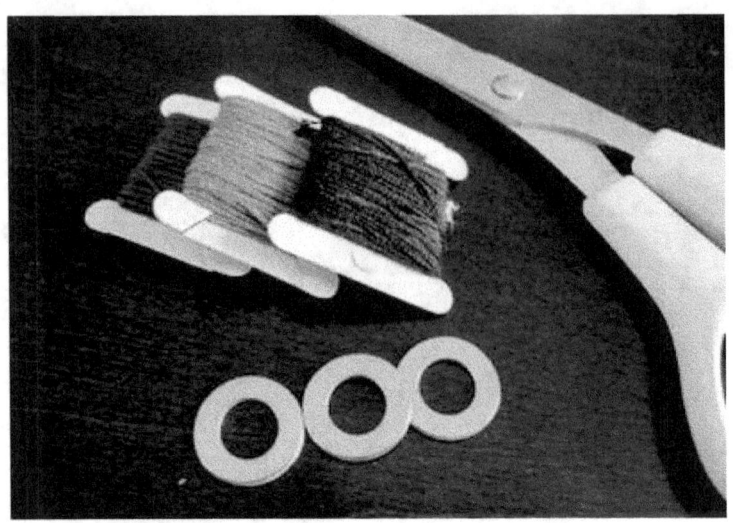

At the end, tie a knot and then cut off the excess thread. To set the end, just add a dab of glue. You can make a few of them in different styles as desired.

Mod Podge® Lace Vases

What you'll need

- Spray paint
- Brush
- Mod Podge® matte
- Various laces
- Various vases

How to make

Wrap a lace accent around the top of your cute little vase, using eyelet fabric or a solid piece of stretch to cover the entire vase.

Then smear Mod Podge® glue onto the vase and put the lace on top, working in increments of a few inches. Keep the lace down and wait for the glue to set the lace in place.

Apply a number of coats of white spray paint to ensure the interior side looks clean and nice.

Continue gluing to cover the vase fully. Ensure that the first piece of your lace meets up evenly with the vase's top. Doing this eliminates the need to trim the fabric later.

Wait for some time to allow the glue to dry and your lace to completely set before you rotate the vase and continue to glue down. At the point where the lace meets up, just trim very closely and glue it down.

Once dry, use Mod Podge® to coat the lace on the vase to ensure it doesn't move. At the end, the lace should be crispy or stiff and thus easy to cut. You can now trim the lace peeking over the vase's bottom.

Recipe Holder Gift Idea

What you'll need

- Clothes pin
- Sandpaper
- Spray paint
- Wood glue
- Drill
- Oval wood piece for base
- Spool
- Finial or top wood piece
- Main wood piece e.g. cabinet door front

How to make

Start by marking the center of your main wood piece on both the top and bottom. Your measurement should be based on the width and thickness of your board.

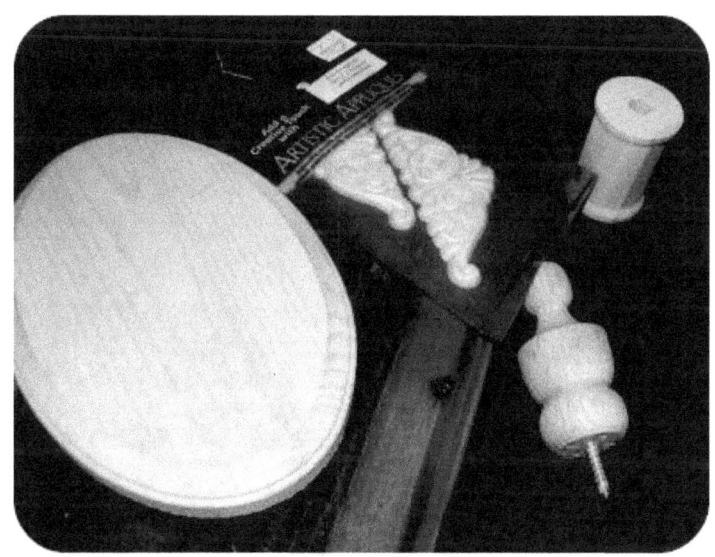

Then drill a hole that is somewhat larger than your screw on the finial. You can even flatten the parts that connect it to the frame using a Forstner bit in case you want to make the holder sturdier with smoother transitions.

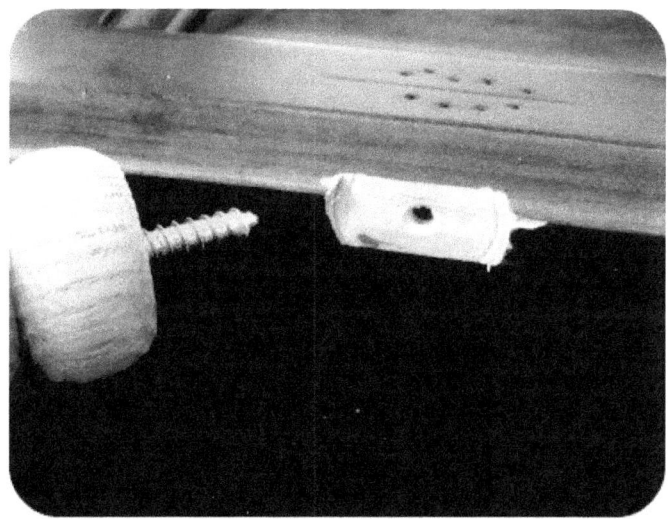

Drill a 3/8 inch hole at the bottom side of the main wood piece or frame, and drill another 3/8 inch hole through the center of the base.

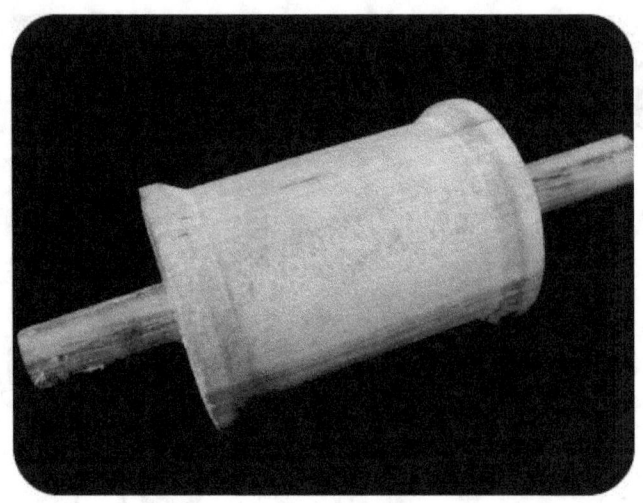

Then cut a 3/8 inch dowel to the required length.

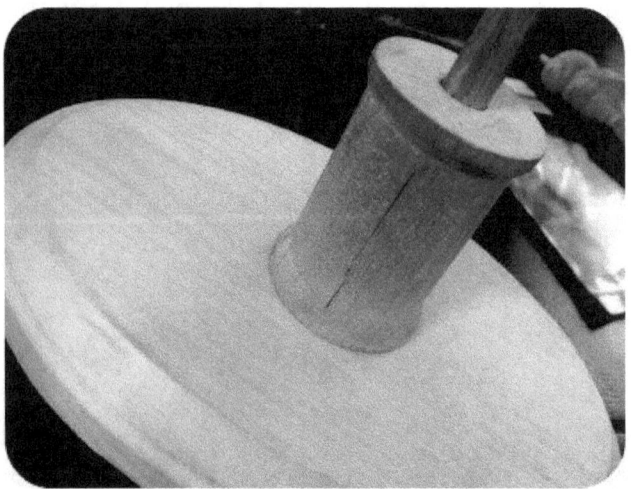

Now apply glue to both the spool and the base. Then push the dowel through and allow to dry.

Apply glue to the hole at the bottom and then push the remainder of the dowel through. Screw the finial on top and spray paint. Allow the paint to dry and apply polyurethane to get a better finish.

At this point, paint the clothespin and allow to dry. You can Mod Podge® scrapbook paper if you like, and hot glue it onto the board.

Tile Coaster Tutorial

What you'll need

- Clear acrylic sealer

- Glue, strong adhesive

- Sponge brush

- Mod Podge®

- 4 pieces of felt (3.75 x 3.75")

- 4 pieces of scrapbook paper (3.75 x 3.75")

- 4 square tiles measuring 4.25 x 4.25"

How to make

First gather your raw materials and then apply Mod Podge® onto one side of the tile using a brush.

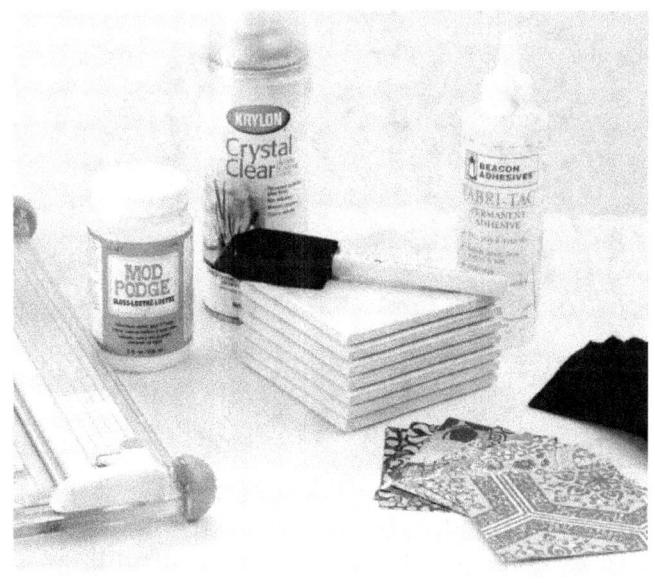

Put one of the pieces of paper on the center of the tile and allow to dry.

Apply another layer of Mod Podge® on the paper and allow about 15 minutes for drying. Then apply 2-3 additional coats.

Once the Mod Podge® is dry, take your tiles outside and spray them with the clear acrylic sealer. The sealer is needed to make the tile coasters waterproof. Follow the manufacturer's directions for best results.

Allow time for the coasters to fully dry and then glue the felt squares to the bottom of the tiles.

Finally wrap up four of the coasters using a good-looking ribbon and your gift is ready.

Conclusion

With these DIY projects and gift ideas, you should be in a position to spread love and probably surprise your mother. Do not be worried if you aren't a very creative designer. You still can manage to develop your own handmade products by following this carefully designed and illustrated tutorial. You only need a few dollars to buy the required components and then get down to work! Just try out the ideas and make this Mother's Day special.

Key Takeaways From This Book

- It's now possible to make plenty of handmade gifts regardless of your skill level. You can actually learn various DIY ideas within a short period.

- You can now utilize your time effectively by studying all the relevant information from one source. You don't have to waste time looking for photos or other details elsewhere.

- Now that you have all the information you need, you just have to purchase the materials you need to make each specific gift.

- When making your gifts, remember that this book is simply a guideline and you can tweak the idea to what is suitable for your mother.

- Don't worry if your gifts don't come out as perfect as you had hoped.

How To Put This Information Into Action

1. Don't spend a lot of money buying materials. Most of the materials you require for these projects are readily available in your own house; you can use old clocks, furniture, or old pieces of metal.

2. Before designing a gift for your mother this year, first decide on the improvements you need to make. You don't need to offer your mom similar gifts just because they seem attractive.

3. To help you keep things interesting, try various consumables that you can offer multiple times without making you appear less creative. Food and other handmade consumables can be very inviting.

4. As indicated earlier, you definitely won't get it right the first time. This means that you need to practice a lot before you can make amazing handmade gifts.

Preview of Essential Oils and Aromatherapy: A Beginner's Guide to Making Essential Oils to Improve Your Mental and Physical Well-Being

Essential Oils for Physical Wellbeing

Using essential oils for skincare and hair care

Essential oil lore is a vast well of knowledge that science has barely touched. There are so many uses of essential oils, with new ones coming out every day. Below are just a few ways you can use essential oils to care for your skin and hair.

Body spray

Combine 5-10 drops of your favorite essential oil with 4 ounces of water in a spray bottle and shake well. Spray as you would a normal body spray.

Note: When using citrus essential oil, don't spray it on your face: citrus oil is photosensitive that makes your skin susceptible to sunburn.

Shampoo

Use lavender cedar wood to treat an itchy scalp by adding a few drops to your shampoo. When you want fuller hair, add rosemary essential oil to your shampoo.

Skin cream

If you want anti-aging support, add two drops of rosemary or rose essential oil to your skin cream.

DIY body oil

Add 5 drops of your favorite skin-safe essential oil to a carrier oil such as olive, borage seed, apricot kernel, wheat germ, or sweet almond. Use liberally every day, and remember to test for skin sensitivity.

In your bathwater

When you are adding essential oils to your bathwater, I strongly suggest you keep away from culinary essential oils such as lemongrass, peppermint, and cinnamon, just to point out a few, because they might cause skin irritation.

To your bathtub, add 5 drops of a skin-safe essential oil.

To download the rest of this book, please click here.

More Books You Might Like

<u>Household DIY: *Save Time and Money with Do It Yourself Hints and Tips on Furniture, Clothes, Pests, Stains, Residues, Odors and More!*</u>

<u>DIY Household Hacks*: Save Time and Money with Do It Yourself Tips and Tricks for Cleaning Your House*</u>

<u>Essential Oils: Essential Oils & Aromatherapy for Beginners: *Proven Secrets to Weight Loss, Skin Care, Hair Care & Stress Relief Using Essential Oil Recipes*</u>

<u>Apple Cider Vinegar for Beginners: *An Apple Cider Vinegar Handbook with Proven Secrets to Natural Weight Loss, Optimum Health and Beautiful Skin*</u>

<u>Body Butter Recipes: *Proven Formula Secrets to Making All Natural Body Butters that Will Hydrate and Rejuvenate Your Skin*</u>

If the links do not work, for whatever reason, you can simply search for these titles on the Amazon website to find them.

Your Free Bonus

As a way of thanking you for your purchase, I'm offering you an opportunity to sign up and be a part of an exclusive book list where members get advanced notice on high-quality books.

To be part of this exclusive club, click on the link below:

https://docs.google.com/forms/d/1ttDqtdRjOeAEtA-BKnq5Hw668vjQS0VWcXCGQ8z9frA/viewform

www.ingramcontent.com/pod-product-compliance
Lightning Source LLC
Chambersburg PA
CBHW071420070526
44578CB00003B/636